KNITTING

Angela Wilkes and Carol Garbera
Illustrated by Lily Whitlock
Designed by Roger Priddy

Cover design by Amanda Barlow.   Cover photography by John Bellenis.
Wool supplied by Creativity.   Border knitted by Sylvia Evans.

CONTENTS

Additional illustrations by John Shackell, Roger Priddy and Christine Berrington.

About this book

Many people know how to knit but have never tried to knit themselves a sweater. This book shows you that knitting is a lot easier than you might think. It gives you patterns for things you will want both to make and wear and shows you what to do as you go along. The patterns start with easy things and progress in difficulty so that by the end of the book you can tackle an Aran sweater.

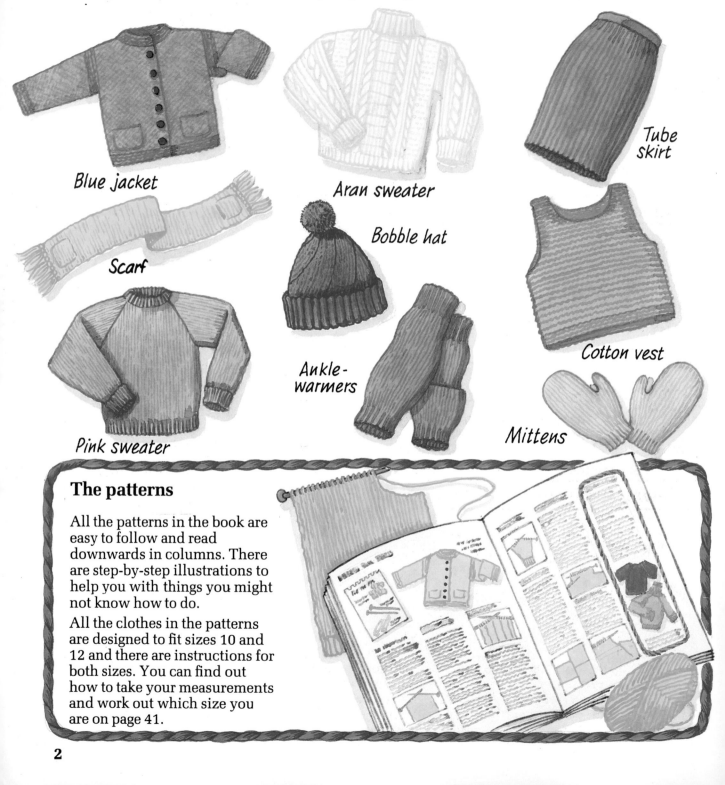

Blue jacket

Aran sweater

Tube skirt

Scarf

Bobble hat

Pink sweater

Ankle-warmers

Cotton vest

Mittens

The patterns

All the patterns in the book are easy to follow and read downwards in columns. There are step-by-step illustrations to help you with things you might not know how to do.

All the clothes in the patterns are designed to fit sizes 10 and 12 and there are instructions for both sizes. You can find out how to take your measurements and work out which size you are on page 41.

Knitting Know How

From this book you can learn the basics of how to knit and also how to do the more fancy stitches, how to knit cables and do circular knitting.

Techniques

You can learn all the basic knitting techniques and skills, such as how to pick up stitches round a neck, or finish off your knitting.

Things you need

On the next few pages you can find out all about the different types of yarn you can buy, knitting needles and other useful things to have.

Following a pattern

Many knitting patterns you buy seem hard to understand at first. On page 12 you can find out how to follow a pattern and what the abbreviations mean.

Making mistakes

Every knitter drops a stitch or makes a mistake from time to time. Don't panic. On page 46 you can find out how to put your mistakes right.

Variations

The first part of each pattern shows you, step-by-step, how to make a basic garment, and at the end of the pattern there are suggestions on how to adapt it. You can find out how to make it longer or shorter, how to alter the basic shape, how to knit it in stripes or knit a number or letter on it. These variations also show you how you can try out and experiment with your own design ideas.

Yarns

There is an enormous choice of yarns available. Some are made from natural fibres, such as wool or cotton, and others from synthetic fibres. Many of the more exotic yarns are made from mixtures of different fibres. Here you can find out about the main types of yarn and what you need to know when buying them.

Natural fibres

Mohair
Warm, thick, fluffy yarn made from goats' wool. Best knitted loosely and made into simple shaped clothes.

Wool
The yarn most commonly used for knitting. Many different types, e.g. Shetland, lambswool and Aran. Easy to knit and keeps its shape well, is warm and does not crease. Needs to be washed carefully.

Fancy yarns
There are many different types. Here are some of the main ones.

slubs

chenille

bouclé

glitter yarns

ribbon / tape

Silk
Very pretty and very expensive. Usually a bit shiny. Is often mixed with wool or cotton to make it cheaper.

Synthetic yarns
These include acrylics, polyesters, nylon and viscose. Strong, light and easy to wash. Not as warm as wool. Often mixed with natural fibres to make stronger, cheaper yarns.

Cotton
Good for summer sweaters. Many types available – plain, fancy, shiny and matt. Sometimes mixed with linen. Hardwearing and easy to wash.

How thick are different yarns?

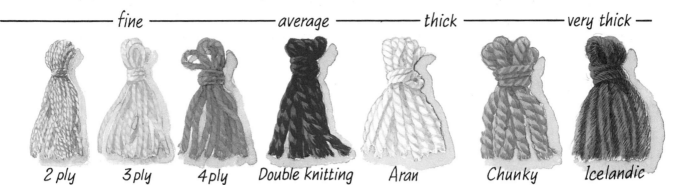

fine —————— average ———— thick —— very thick

2 ply   3 ply   4 ply   Double knitting   Aran   Chunky   Icelandic

Yarns are made of spun fibres, called plys, which are twisted together. A 3 ply yarn, for example, contains three strands of fibre. The number of plys does not necessarily tell you how thick the yarn is as the plys can be thick or thin, depending on the types of yarn. This is a rough guide to which types of yarn are fine and which ones are thick.

About your yarn

Knitting patterns always tell you how much yarn you need. Yarn is sold by weight. Every ball of yarn has a paper label which tells you how much it weighs and gives you other useful information.

The yarn label tells you what the yarn is made of and where it was made.

It also gives you washing instructions for the yarn. Always keep a label for future reference.

This symbol shows you what size needles to use.

This number refers to the colour of the yarn. If you want to know which colours are available in a particular yarn, ask the shop assistant to show you the shade chart.

Yarn is dyed in batches or 'lots' and always has a lot number. Every time a new lot is dyed, the dye is made again, so it varies a little from one lot to another. Make sure that all the yarn you buy for any one garment has the same lot number.

Things you need

All you need to start knitting is a pair of needles and some yarn, but there are different types of needles for different types of knitting. Below you can find out what they are.

There are also some gadgets which can help to make knitting easier. You can read about them on the opposite page.

Single-pointed needles

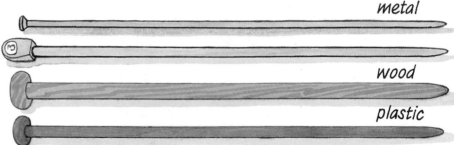

metal

wood

plastic

These are the needles you usually knit with. They are sized according to how thick they are. The thicker the needle, the bigger the stitches it makes. You can buy long or short knitting needles. The shorter ones are usually easier to use unless you are knitting something with a lot of stitches.

Cable needle

You use this to hold a group of stitches when you are knitting cables. It should be the same size or smaller than the other needles you are using.

Double pointed needles

These come in normal sizes, in sets of six or four. You use them to knit small, tubular things without a seam, such as polo necks or socks.

Circular needle

You use a circular needle to knit seamless, tubular things, such as skirts. You can buy them in different lengths, so check what your pattern says.

Needle sizes

Nowadays you buy needles in metric sizes, but many people still have needles in English sizes. In this chart you can see which sizes correspond to which.

Continental (mm)	2¼	2¾	3	3¼	3¾	4	4½	5	5½	6	6½	7	7½	8½	9
English	13	12	11	10	9	8	7	6	5	4	3	2	1	00	000
U.S.	0	1	2	3	4	5	6	7	8	9	10	10½	11	13	15

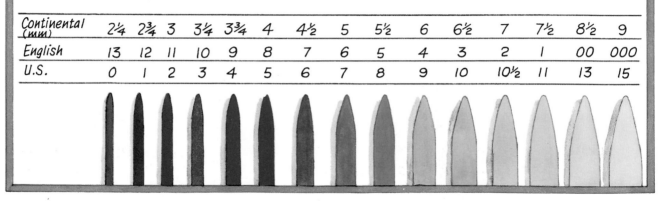

Other useful things

Stitch holder

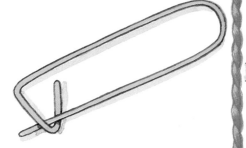

Like a giant safety pin. On it you keep stitches which you are not knitting, until you are ready to knit them. It is a good idea to have at least two.

Row counter

This helps you to keep track of how many rows you have knitted. You slip it on to the end of a needle and turn it as you finish each row.

Needle guards

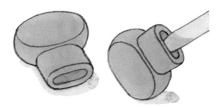

You put these on the points of your needles when you are not knitting so that you do not drop stitches. They also help protect your knitting bag.

Tapestry or darning needles

Large, blunt-ended needles like these are best for sewing up your pieces of knitting.

Long pins

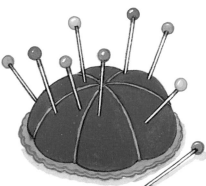

For pinning your knitting out before pressing it or sewing it together.

Small sharp scissors

For cutting yarn and trimming loose yarn ends.

Tape measure

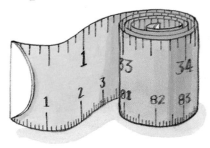

To check your tension is right (see page 13) and to measure your knitting.

Crochet hook

For picking up dropped stitches.

Knitting gauge

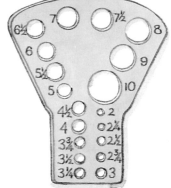

You can use this to check the metric sizes of your knitting needles and crochet hooks.

Starting to knit

Making the first row of stitches on a needle is called casting on. There are many ways to cast on, but the way shown here is easy and gives knitting a firm edge.

The two main knitting stitches are called knit and purl. If you have not knitted before, find a pair of needles and some leftover yarn. Cast on 20 stitches and practise doing knit and purl before you try to knit anything.

Casting on

Wind the yarn round your finger and pull a loop through it. Slip it on to a knitting needle and pull it to make a stitch.

Hold this needle in your left hand. Put your right needle into the stitch and wind the yarn under and around it.

How to knit

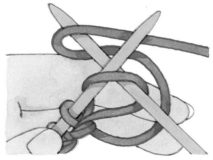

With the yarn at the back, slip the right needle into the first stitch on the left needle. Wind the yarn around it as shown.

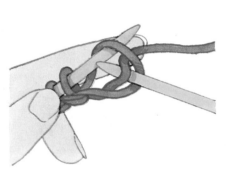

Pull the loop of yarn towards you through the stitch on the left needle.

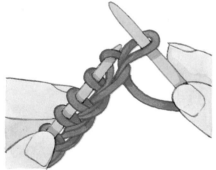

Push the right needle forwards and slide the old stitch off the left needle, keeping the new stitch on the right needle.

How to purl

With the yarn at the front, put the right needle into the front of the first stitch on the left needle, from right to left.

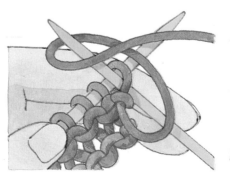

Wind the yarn over and around the point of the right needle anticlockwise, as shown.

Pull the loop of yarn backwards through the stitch on the left needle and push the old stitch towards the tip of the needle.

Then pull a loop through with the point of the right needle to make a stitch and slip it on to the left needle.

To make the next stitch, put the right needle between the two stitches, wind the yarn around it and carry on as before.

Make the rest of the stitches in the same way. Start each one by putting the needle between the two last stitches.

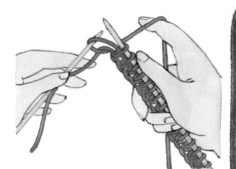

Carry on to the end of the row. To start a new row, turn the knitting round and hold the full needle in your left hand.

How to hold the needles and yarn

If you thread the yarn between your fingers when knitting, it helps you to knit faster and more evenly.

Holding the yarn in your right hand

Holding the yarn in your left hand

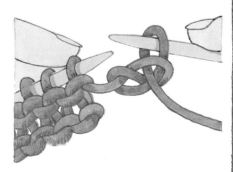

Slide the old stitch off the end of the left needle, keeping the new stitch on the right needle. Carry on like this along the row.

You use your right forefinger to wind the yarn round the needles.

You use your left forefinger to wind the yarn round the needles.

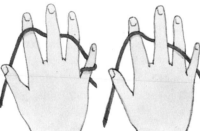

9

The basic stitches

All knitting stitches are made up of knit and purl used in different combinations. Here are the main stitches you need to know. They are used in most of the patterns in this book.

To practise them, use odd scraps of double knitting yarn and size 4mm needles. Cast on 20 stitches and knit 20 rows, then cast off. You can see how to do this at the bottom of the page.

Garter stitch

The easiest stitch to do. Just knit every stitch of every row. (You can also do it by purling every stitch of every row).

Stocking stitch

Knit one row, then purl one row throughout. Looks like jersey on the right side and fine garter stitch on the wrong side.

Ribbing 1

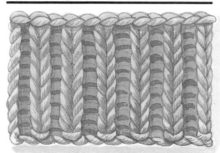

Knit 1, bring yarn forwards, purl 1, take yarn back. Repeat these 2 stitches to end of row. On the next row, knit the purl stitches and purl the knit ones.

Ribbing 2

Knit 2, bring yarn forwards, purl 2, take yarn back. Repeat these 4 stitches to end of row. On the next row, knit the purl stitches and purl the knit ones.

Moss stitch

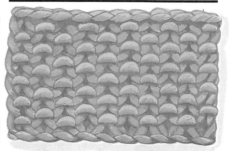

Knit one, bring yarn forwards, purl one, take yarn back. Repeat to end of row. On the next row, knit the knit stitches and purl the purl stitches.

How to cast off

When you have finished your knitting, you "cast off". This means that you knit the stitches off the needle to make a neat edge which does not come undone.

It is best to cast off on a knit row, but if you do cast off on a purl row, purl all of the stitches instead of knitting them. When casting off ribbing, keep to the rib pattern and use both knit and purl. Always cast off loosely.

Knit the first two stitches in the row. With the yarn at the back of the work, put the left needle into the first stitch.

Lift the first stitch over the second one, as shown, and drop it off the needle so that only the second stitch is left.

Knitting Hints

These hints should help you if you are just starting to knit.

Try to knit evenly. The stitches should be just loose enough for you to put a needle into them easily.

If you are a beginner knitter, count your stitches at the end of every row, to check that you have not dropped one.

Do not worry if you have dropped a stitch or made a mistake. You can find out how to put mistakes right on p. 46.

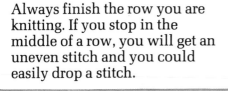

Always finish the row you are knitting. If you stop in the middle of a row, you will get an uneven stitch and you could easily drop a stitch.

Knitting quickly comes with practise, so always try to knit a few rows at a time. If you want to knit something quick, choose something small that you knit on big needles.

Keep your knitting and all your knitting things together in a bag so that you do not lose anything. It will also help to keep your knitting clean.

Knit another stitch, then lift the first stitch over the second one as before. Carry on like this along the row.

When you reach the last stitch, break off the yarn, slip it through the stitch and pull it, to tighten the loop.

When you finish off your knitting, thread the end of yarn on to a darning needle and darn it into the edge of the knitting.

Following a pattern

Knitting patterns often seem difficult to read. The patterns in this book have been clearly laid out under different headings so that they are easy to follow. Here you can find out what each part of the pattern tells you. In the column on the right you will find a list of the abbreviations most commonly used in knitting patterns.

This tells you which type of yarn and what size needles to use. It also tells you if there is anything else you need – such as stitch holders or buttons.

Tension

This tells you how many stitches and rows you should have to each centimeter you knit. You can find out more about this on the opposite page.

Measurements

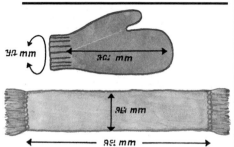

The diagram shows you what the measurements of the finished garment should be.

Sizes

In patterns for two sizes, the smaller size, or the figures that apply to it, are printed first, and the larger size comes after it in brackets.

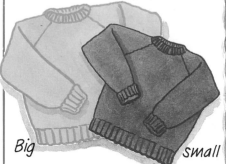

Big   Small

Where there is just one figure, it applies to both sizes. If you underline the figures that apply to your size before you start, you will be able to pick them out more easily as you knit.

Method

The knitting instructions are written in columns. Whenever you stop knitting, make a pencil mark on the pattern, so you do not lose your place.

Making up

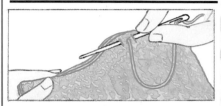

This tells you how to finish off what you are making and how to sew it up. You can find out more about this on pages 44/45.

Abbreviations

This list covers all the most common knitting abbreviations. You can find out more about the terms used on the page numbers shown.

beg	beginning
cm	centimetre
cont	continue
dec	decrease (p.43)
garter st	garter stitch (p.10)
inc	increase (p.42)
k	knit
k2tog	knit 2 stitches together (p.43)
kwise	knitwise (insert needle as if to knit)
m1	make 1 (p.43)
p	purl
psso	pass slip stitch over
pwise	purlwise (insert needle as if to purl)
rem	remaining
rep	repeat
sl	slip a stitch to the other needle without knitting it.
st	stitch
st st	stocking stitch
tbl	through back of loop
tog	together

Asterisks

Asterisks mark a pattern section that has to be repeated. "Repeat from * to end" means you have to keep repeating the pattern section to the end of the row.

Knitting things the right size

If you want the things you knit to finish up the right size, your knitting must be the right tightness or "tension". If you knit too tightly, your knitting will end up too small.

If you knit too loosely, your garment will end up too big.

The type of yarn, size of needle and stitch you use all affect the size of your knitting.

Every knitting pattern gives you the tension for that pattern. Always check your tension using the recommended yarn before you start knitting. It does not take long and can save a lot of disappointment later.

How to check your tension

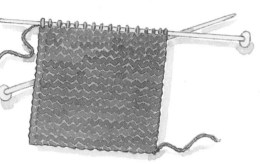

Knit a sample square, using the right yarn, needles and stitch. It is best to make it a little bigger than the tension given in the pattern. For example, if the pattern says 22 sts and 32 rows = 10 cm, cast on 26 stitches and knit 36 rows, then cast off.

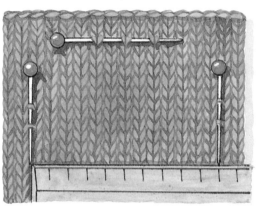

Smooth the square out on a flat surface without stretching it, then mark out a 10 cm square with pins. Lay a tape measure across the knitting and count every stitch and half stitch between the pins. Count the rows in the same way.

Too loose or too tight?

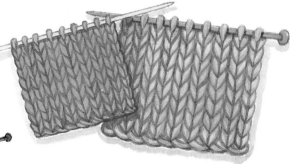

If there are too many stitches and rows in the pinned area, your knitting is too tight. Knit another sample with needles a size larger. If there are too few stitches and rows, your knitting is too loose. Knit a square with needles a size smaller.

Ankle warmers

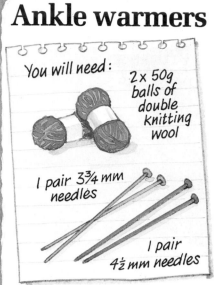
Tension

20 sts and 29 rows – 10cm in st st using size 4½mm needles.

Method

With size 3¾mm needles cast on 58 sts and knit 4cm in k1,p1 rib.

Change to 4½mm needles. Cont in stocking stitch until work measures 28cm from beginning.

Change back to 3¾mm needles and knit 6cm in k1,p1 rib. Cast off loosely. Knit the 2nd anklewarmer in the same way.

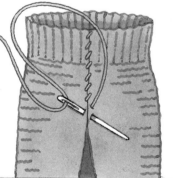

Making up

Lightly press wrong side of stocking stitch*. Fold anklewarmers in half lengthways, right sides together. Sew up side seams, using a flat seam.

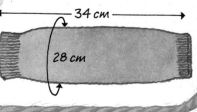

Turn the anklewarmers the right way out. Wear them with the longer ribbing at the top.

Measurements

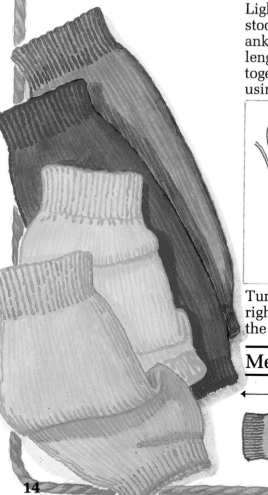

34 cm

28 cm

Mittens

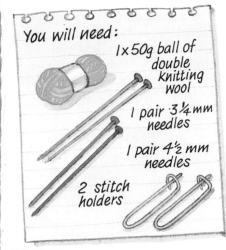
Tension

As for anklewarmers

Method

With size 3¼mm needles cast on 40 sts and work in k2,p2 rib for 6cm.

Change to 4½mm needles. Starting with a knit row, work 2 rows st st.

Next row K19, k twice into next st, k twice into next st, k19 – 42 sts.

Work 3 rows in st st, starting with a purl row.

Next row K19, k twice into next st, k2, k twice into next st, k19 – 44 sts.

Starting with a purl row, cont straight in st st for 7 rows. Break off wool.

Thumb

Slip the first 16 sts on to a stitch holder.

Rejoin wool and knit next 12 sts.

Slip the last 16 sts on to a stitch holder.

Next row Purl twice into first st, p11, p twice into last st – 14sts.

Starting with a k row, work straight in st st for 14 rows.

14

* See p.44

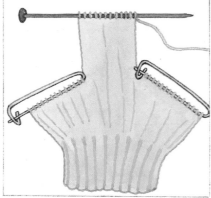

Shape top of thumb

1st row K2tog along row – 7sts.
2nd row P2tog 3 times, p1–7sts.
Break wool, thread it through
rem sts with a darning needle
and sew it firmly.

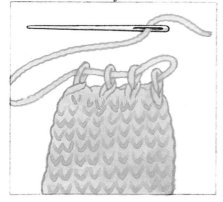

Hand

Rejoin wool to right side. Knit
16 sts on 1st stitch holder, pick
up 1st st from each side of base
of thumb, k16 sts on 2nd holder
– 34sts. Cont in st st until work
measures 21.5cm from beg.

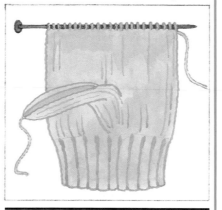

Shape top of hand

1st row K2tog, k13, k2tog,
k2tog, k13, k2tog – 30 sts.
2nd, 4th, 6th row Purl
3rd row K2tog, k11, k2tog,
k2tog, k11, k2tog – 26sts.
5th row K2tog, k9, k2tog, k2tog,
k9, k2tog.
7th row Cast off.

Making up

Lightly press stocking stitch on
wrong side. Fold mittens in
half, right sides together. Sew
up thumbs with flat seams,
using the thread left at the top
of it. Sew up outside seams of
mitten, using a flat seam. Turn
mittens right way out and press.

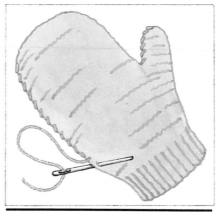

Measurements

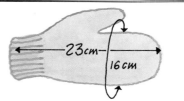

Scarf with pockets

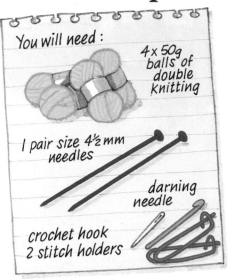

You will need:

4 x 50g balls of double knitting

1 pair size 4½mm needles

darning needle

crochet hook
2 stitch holders

This scarf is knitted in easy garter stitch. You can knit it in a plain colour with pockets or make it striped.

Tension

20sts and 32 rows = 10cm in garter stitch, using size 4½mm needles.

Length excluding tassels

112cm

Width: 22.5cm

Pocket

With size 4½mm needles cast on 22 sts and knit 11cm of garter st. Leave the sts on a stitch holder.

Main piece

Cast on 48 sts and work in garter st for 12cm. If you slip the 1st stitch in every row without knitting it, it will give the scarf firm edges.

Joining yarn

When you finish a ball of yarn, join the new one at the beginning of a row. Hold the two ends of yarn together and knit the row with the new yarn only. Tie the ends together when you have finished the row.

Adding the pocket

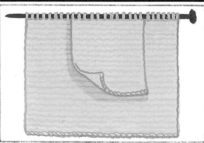

Next row K13, cast off next 22 sts, k to end of row.
Next row K13, knit across the 22 sts at the top of the pocket, k to end of row.
Continue straight until work measures 99cm from beginning.

Second pocket

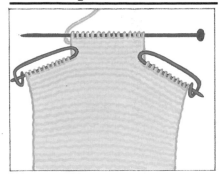

Knit 13 sts and put them on a holder, k22, put the last 13 sts on to a holder. Cont straight on rem 22 sts for 11cm. Cast off.

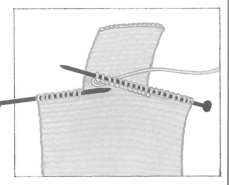

With right side facing you, rejoin wool. Slip the first 13 sts back on to needle. Cast on 22 sts, then knit 2nd group of 13 sts (48 sts altogether). Cont straight for 12cm. Cast off.

Making Up

Neatly sew the loose ends of wool into the sides of the scarf and sew them firmly in place with small stitches.

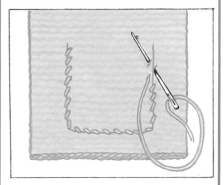

Sew the two pockets in place. Lay them flat against the wrong side of the scarf, then carefully oversew the three free sides. Sew the ends of yarn firmly in place with small stitches.

Making the tassels

Wind wool around a small book, then cut down one side to make lengths of wool. You need 180 lengths about 20cm long. Divide them into groups of 10.

Fold 10 lengths of wool in half and pull them through the bottom edge of the scarf, from front to back, with a crochet hook. Pull the ends firmly through the loop to make a knotted tassel.

Make 9 tassels at each end of the scarf and trim the ends.

Striped scarf

To knit a scarf in two colours you need 2 x 50g balls of each colour.

Fine stripes

Leave out the pockets and work alternate stripes two rows deep. When knitting the stripes, carry the colour not being used loosely up the side of the work until it is needed. Make the tassels in alternate colours.

Wide stripes

Knit each stripe 10cm deep. Join the colour for each new stripe as you would a new ball of wool.

Bobble hat

You will need:
3 x 50g balls double knitting wool

1 pair 3¼ mm needles
1 pair 4½ mm needles

piece of card 8cm x 16cm

scissors
darning needle

Measurements

56 cm

25 cm

Tension

20 sts and 29 rows = 10cm in stocking stitch, using size 4½mm needles.

Method

With 3¼mm needles cast on 120 sts and work in k2,p2 rib for 11cm. Change to 4½mm needles and cont in st st, starting with a k row, until hat measures 16cm from beginning.

Shaping

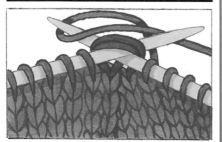

Row 1 *K13, k2tog, rep from * to end of row (112 sts).
Row 2 and every alternate row Purl
Row 3 *Knit 12, k2tog, rep from * to end of row (104 sts).
Carry on decreasing on every knit row, with one less st between decreases each time until you have knitted 12 rows from beg of shaping (72 sts).

Row 13 *Knit 7, k2tog, rep from * to end of row (64 sts).
Next row P2tog*, p6, sl1, p1, psso, rep from * to end of row
Next row *Knit 5, k2tog, rep from * to end of row
Next row Purl
Repeat the last 2 rows, decreasing on every k row with one less st between the decreases each row until there are 16 sts left, ending with a purl row.

Top of the hat

Next row K2tog all along row (8sts).
Next row P2tog all along row (4sts).
Break wool and thread it through the last 4 sts with a darning needle.

Making Up

Lay the hat over the end of an ironing board and lightly press the st st area on the wrong side.

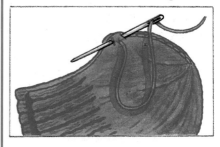

Fold the hat in half, right sides together. Sew the wool left at the top of the hat firmly in place, then backstitch the side seam as far as the ribbing. Turn the hat right side out and sew up the ribbing with a flat seam.

Making the bobble

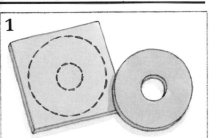

1

Draw 2 circles 7cm in diameter on card. In the centre of each circle draw a circle 2cm across. Cut them out to make two rings.

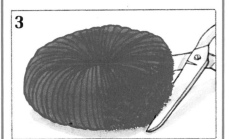

2

Put the two card rings together and wind wool evenly round them. Use a darning needle to do this when the hole is small.

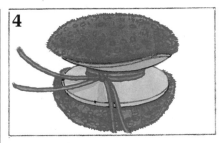

3

When the hole is full, cut round the edges of the circles through all the layers of wool between the card rings.

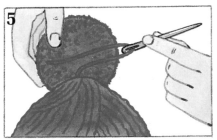

4

Ease the card rings apart and tie a double length of wool tightly round the middle of the bobble. Leave the long ends free.

5

Remove the card rings and fluff out the bobble. Use the long ends of wool to sew the bobble on top of the hat.

How to knit stripes

You can make a striped hat, mittens or anklewarmers. Here are the amounts of yarn you will need and some ideas for different types of narrow stripes.

Mittens

2 × 50g balls double knitting wool in contrasting colours.

Work 2 rows st st in each colour in turn. Carry the colour not being used up the side of the work until needed.

Hat

2 × 50g balls main colour
1 × 50g ball contrast colour

Work 4 rows st st in one colour, then 2 rows in the other. Repeat to end. Make the bobble out of both colours.

Anklewarmers

2 × 50g balls main colour
1 × 50g ball contrast colour

Work 4 rows st st in each colour in turn. Backstitch the seams so the loops do not show on right side of work.

You can check how to decrease on page 43.

Cotton vest

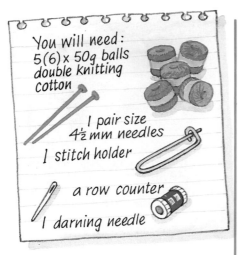

You will need:
5(6) x 50g balls double knitting cotton

1 pair size 4½ mm needles

1 stitch holder

a row counter

1 darning needle

Tension

19 sts and 30 rows = 10cm in ridge stitch pattern, using size 4½mm needles.

Size

To fit 81 (86)cm/32"(34") chest. Figures in brackets are for the larger size.

Front

Cast on 76(80)sts and work 6 rows in garter st. Then work in ridge pattern, as follows:
Row 1 Knit
Row 2 Purl
Row 3 Knit
Row 4 Knit
Repeat these 4 rows until you have worked 19(21) ridges.

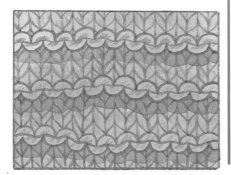

Shaping the armholes

Continuing in ridge pattern, cast off 6 sts at beginning of next 2 rows – 64(68) sts, then k2tog at each end of every row until there are 48(52 sts) left, ending with a p row.
Cont straight for 21(25) rows, but from now on knit the first and last 4 sts on every purl row to make garter st edges. *

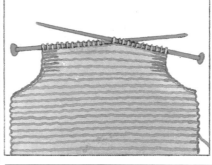

Neck shaping

Next row (row 4 of pattern)
Knit 18(19), then slip these sts on to a stitch holder. Cast off 12(14 sts), then knit the remaining 18(19) sts.

Left shoulder

Shape the left shoulder on the remaining 18(19) sts, as follows:
Row 1 K16(17), k2tog.
Row 2 K4, p9(10), k4.
Row 3 K15(16), k2tog.
Row 4, 8, 12 Knit.
Row 5 K14(15), k2tog.
Row 6 K4, p7(8), k4.
Row 7 K13(14), k2tog.
Row 9 K12(13), k2tog.
Row 10 K4, p5(6), k4.
Row 11 K11(12), k2tog.
Row 13 K10(11), k2tog.
Row 14 K4, p3(4), k4.
Row 15 K9(10), k2tog (10, 11 sts).

Cont straight in garter st for 16 rows. Cast off.

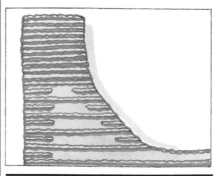

Right shoulder

Rejoin yarn to remaining 18(19) sts. Starting on right side, knit as for left shoulder but reverse the shaping by decreasing (k2tog) at the beginning, not the end, of every right side row.

Back

Work as for Front as far as *, then cont straight in pattern for another 8 rows before starting to shape neck. When neck shaping is finished, only work 8 rows garter st at top of shoulder.

Making up

Sew in the loose ends. Pin the side seams right sides together, matching the ridges. Backstitch neatly. Flat seam shoulder

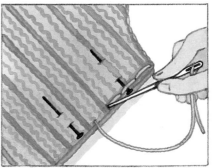

straps together. Press seams lightly on wrong side.

This summery vest is quick and easy to make

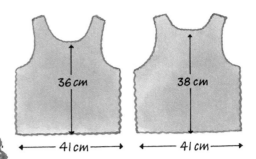

36 cm

← 41 cm →

38 cm

← 41 cm →

Colour variation

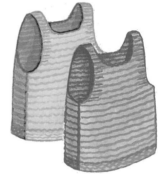

You will need 3 × 50g balls in 2 contrasting colours (6 balls altogether). Knit Front in one colour and Back in the other.

Mini summer top

You will need 5 × 50g balls of double knitting cotton. Only work 13 ridges before starting armhole shaping.

Hip length version

You will need 7 × 50g balls of double knitting cotton. Follow instructions for the larger size and work 24 ridges before shaping the armholes.

Striped vest

You will need 5 × 50g balls in main colour and 1 × 50g ball in contrast colour (both sizes).

Knit the garter st hem, then knit a band of contrast colour for 6 ridges (24 rows). Do the same for Back and Front.

Tube skirt

Measurements

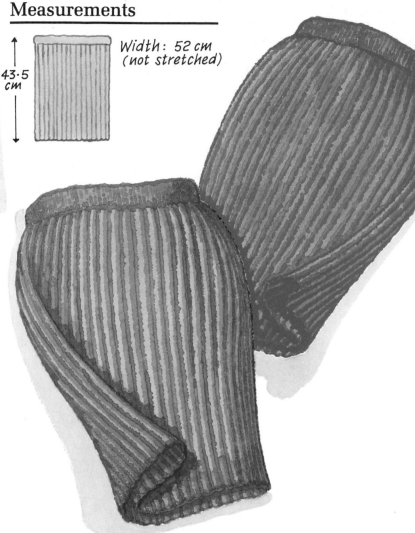

43.5 cm

Width: 52 cm (not stretched)

Knitting in the round

This skirt is knitted on a circular needle, so it does not have a seam. To knit in the round, you use a long, bendy double-ended needle. You cast on, then just keep knitting in the same direction, with the right side facing you.

Size

One size to fit hip size 88cm (34½ inches)

Method

Cast on 200 sts, using the ends of the circular needle as a pair. Tie a piece of coloured thread round the wool after the last st, to make a marker.

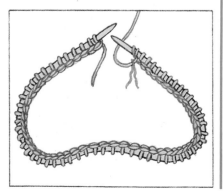

Start working in k2, p2 rib. To start the first row, knit the first stitch as shown, pulling the yarn tightly so there is no gap where the tube is joined.

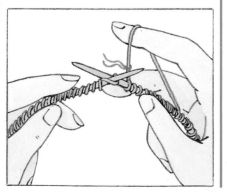

At the end of the row, carry straight on round to start the 2nd row. Cont in rib until work measures 40cm from beg, ending in line above the marker.

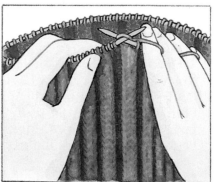

Decrease row

Next row Continuing in rib, decrease 1 st every 5 sts all along the row (knit 2 together or purl 2 together, depending on which type of stitch comes first) – you should have 160 sts left at the end of the row.

Waistband

Knit every row for 6cm. As you are knitting in the round, this will look like stocking stitch. Make sure you finish the last row in line with the marker, then cast off loosely.

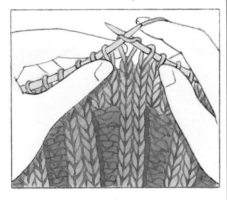

Making up

Fold waistband in half to wrong side of knitting and oversew the cast off edge to the decrease row, as shown, to make a casing. Leave a 4cm opening for the elastic.

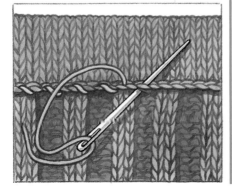

Fasten the safety pin to one end of the elastic and thread it through the waist casing, being careful not to twist it.

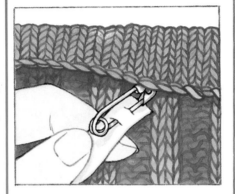

Pin the ends of the elastic together, then try the skirt on and adjust the elastic to fit your waist comfortably. Sew the ends of the elastic together firmly. Oversew the opening left in the waistband.

Long skirt

You will need 8 × 50g balls double knitting wool.

Knit as for short skirt, only knit 60cm of ribbing before the decrease row.

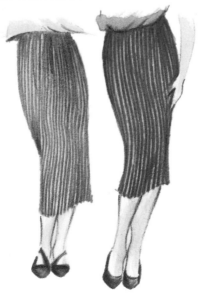

Striped skirts

Short version

You will need
1 × 50g balls in 5 colours
or
3 x 50g balls in 2 colours

Long version

You will need
1 × 50g ball in 8 colours
or
4 × 50g balls in 2 colours

Knit as for basic pattern, but knit 10cm stripes, using either 2 colours alternately or by making each stripe a different colour. Change the colours exactly in line with the hem marker thread each time, as the join will show slightly and should be straight. Darn in the loose ends before finishing.

Pink sweater

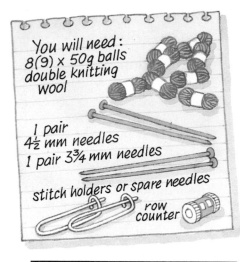

You will need :
8(9) x 50g balls
double knitting
wool

1 pair
4½ mm needles
1 pair 3¾ mm needles

stitch holders or spare needles

row counter

Tension

21 sts and 29 rows = 10cm in st st using 4½mm needles.

Size

To fit 81(86)cm/32(34) inch chest

Back

With size 3¾mm needles cast on 85(90) sts and work in k1, p1 rib for 7cm.
Next row Increase into 1st st, then every 12th st along the row, 92(98) sts. Change to size 4½mm needles and work in st st for 33(35)cm, ending with a purl row. Mark each end of the row with a thread. (To show where to position the sleeves when you sew them in later.)

Armhole shaping

Cast off 2 sts at beginning of next 2 rows, then decrease 1 st at each end of every knit row until there are 26 sts left. Leave these sts on a spare needle.

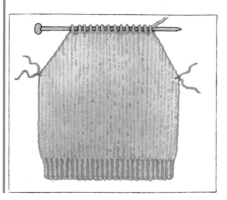

The pattern for this raglan sleeve sweater starts on this page and on the next few pages you will find lots of interesting ways to adapt the basic pattern.

Baggy mohair

Letter on front

Striped

Front

Work as for Back, including armhole shaping, until 47 sts left. Finish with a purl row.

Neck shaping

K2tog, k14 and slip the rest of the sts on to a stitch holder. Work left side of neck on remaining 15 sts, as follows:
Row 1 P2tog, p to end.
Row 2 K2tog, k to last 2 sts, k2 tog.
Repeat these 2 rows once.
Row 5 P2tog, p to end – 8 sts.
Continue decreasing at armhole edge on every k row until there is 1 st left. Cast off.

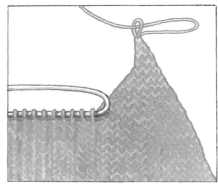

Leave middle 14(15) sts on stitch holder. Slip remaining 16 sts on to a needle. With right side of work facing you, rejoin wool to the sts on the needle. Knit as far as last 2 sts, k2tog.

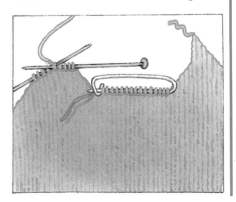

Work right side of neck as follows:
Row 1 P to last 2 sts, p2tog.
Row 2 K2tog, k to last 2 sts, k2tog.
Repeat these 2 rows once.
Row 5 P to last 2 sts, p2tog.
Continue decreasing at armhole edge on every k row until there is 1 st left. Cast off.

Sleeves

With size 3¾mm needles cast on 37(41) sts and work in k1, p1 rib for 15cm.
Next row Increase into 1st st and every 4th st after that – 46(52) sts.
Change to size 4½mm needles and cont in st st. Increase 1 st at each end of every 8th row until there are 69(74) sts. Cont straight until work measures 50(53)cm from beg, ending with a purl row.

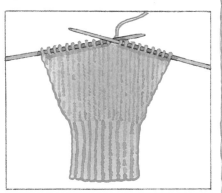

Armhole shaping

Cast off 2 sts at beg of next 2 rows, then dec 1 st at each end of every 4th row until there are 59(61) sts left. Then dec at each end of every k row until there are 7 sts left. Put these on a spare needle or stitch holder.

Knit the second sleeve in exactly the same way.

Measurements

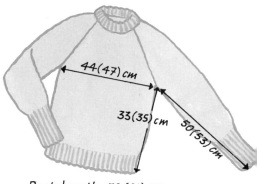

44(47) cm

33(35) cm   50(53) cm

Back length : 58 (61) cm

Things to remember

To increase

Knit twice into the same stitch (see p.42). At the end of a row, knit twice into the 2nd to last stitch.

To decrease

Knit two stitches together on a knit row, and purl two stitches together on a purl row (see p.43)

25

Pink sweater 2

Neckband

With the right side of the knitting facing you, pick up the stitches round the neck with a size 3¾mm needle. Knit the 26 stitches left at the top of the Back.

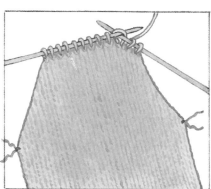

Knit the 7 sts at the top of one sleeve, then pick up 14 sts down the side of the Front neck, as shown at bottom of page. Knit the centre 14(15) sts of the neck, pick up the 14 sts back to the shoulder and knit across the 7 sts at the top of second sleeve. You should have 82(83) sts altogether. Knit 6cm of k1, p1 rib and leave the sts on the needle.

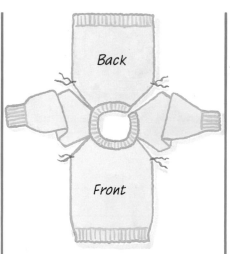

Sewing the neckband

Turn the knitting inside out. Thread a length of yarn on to a darning needle and make a couple of firm stitches at the base of the neckband.

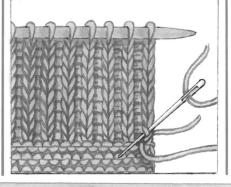

Fold the neckband in half, to the wrong side of the knitting, and loosely sew each stitch from the needle in turn to the first row of the ribbing.

By sewing the neckband down like this you get a firm but stretchy neckband that you can pull over your head easily.

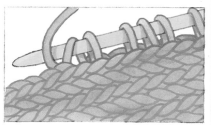

How to pick up stitches along an edge

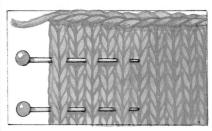

When you pick up new stitches, try to space them evenly or the edge will pucker. Aim to pick up 3 stitches out of every 4 row ends.

Hold the knitting in your left hand and the needle and yarn in your right hand. Put the needle between the 1st and 2nd sts in from the edge.

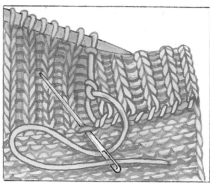

Wind the yarn round the needle, as if doing a knit stitch, and pull the loop through to make a new stitch. Repeat along the edge.

"Blocking" the knitting

Before you press a sweater, it is a good idea to shape it by pinning each piece in turn out to the right size. Knitters call this 'blocking'. It may seem fiddly, but it is well worth the trouble as you will find it easier to sew up your knitting and the finished result will look very professional. Remember to sew in all the loose yarn ends before you press your knitting.

To block knitting you need a firm, padded surface, so cover a table with a folded blanket or thick towels.

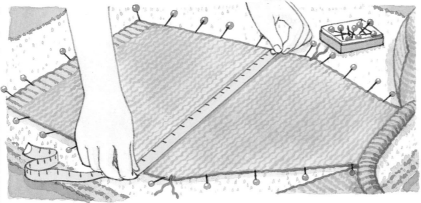

Lay the knitting, right side down, on top and smooth each piece out to the measurements given in the pattern and pin the edges down, as shown. Be careful not to stretch the knitting and make sure the rows run in straight lines.

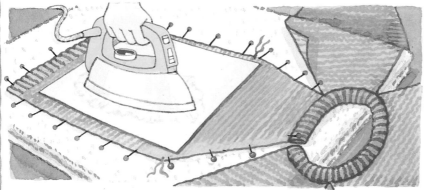

Gently press the knitting, a bit at a time, using a damp cloth and warm iron. Only press the stocking stitch areas, not the ribbing*. Leave the knitting on the table until it has cooled and dried, then you can take out the pins.

Sewing up the sweater

Pin the sleeves into the armholes, right sides together, above the marker threads and backstitch the shoulder seams.

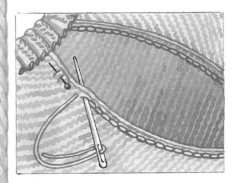

Backstitch the underarm sleeve seams and side seams as far as the cuff and hem ribbing. Flat seam the cuffs and ribbing.

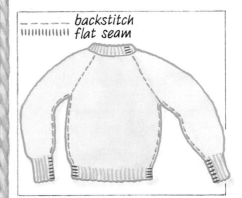

- - - - - backstitch
|||||||||| flat seam

Flat seam the ends of the neckband together. Press the seams lightly and fold the cuffs back on the right side.

*See page 44 for how to press knitting and page 45 on ways of sewing up seams.

Striped sweater

You can knit the basic sweater in stripes. Here are some ideas for different types of stripe and you can find more on page 19. It is best to keep stripes simple and knit them all the same width. Knit a sample before you start, to check that the colours you have chosen go well together, and write down how many rows there are in each colour.

Joining new colours

If you are knitting narrow stripes in 2 or 3 colours you can carry a colour you are not using loosely up the side of the knitting until needed, then twist it round the previous colour before you start the new row.

For wide stripes, break off the wool and join the new colour as you would a new ball of wool (see page 16).

Yarn quantities

For narrow stripes on a background colour you will need 7 × 50g balls in the main colour (including ribbing) and 2 × 50g balls in the contrast colours.

If you are using 2 colours in equal stripes you will need 2 × 50g balls of the ribbing colour + 4 × 50g balls in each of the 2 colours for the stripes.

You can use up leftover wool as long as it is all the same type of wool and you have enough. Weigh it and check that you have at least 450g.

Matching stripes

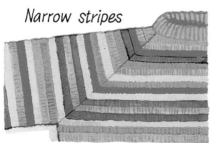

Narrow stripes

Make sure that the stripes match on the body and sleeves by starting the raglan shaping on the sleeves and the body on the same colour stripe.

Wide stripes

Work out how many stripes fit in here

Then work out how many fit in here

Decide how wide to make the stripes and work out from the pattern measurements how many will fit between the ribbing and armholes on the Back and Front. Then work out from the armhole down how many stripes will fit on the sleeves. Write down how many stripes there are on each piece.

Baggy square sweater

You can knit this loose, boxy sweater by following the basic sweater pattern and leaving out the ribbing. The edges of the sweater will roll outwards slightly as you wear it and cover the cast-on and cast-off stitches. The chest and length measurements will be the same as for the basic sweater.

You will need 9 × 50g balls of double knitting wool and a pair of size 4½mm needles.

Back and Front

Follow the instructions for the larger size sweater, but do not knit the ribbing. Cast on 97 stitches for the front and back, then work in stocking stitch, following the pattern from the top of the ribbing onwards. You will need to knit 42cm up to the beginning of the armhole shaping, as there is no ribbing. Cast off the stitches at the top of the Back and Front.

Sleeves

Cast on 50 stitches, then follow the pattern instructions from the beginning of the stocking stitch onwards. Cast off the stitches left at the top of the sleeves.

Making up

Do not knit a neckband. Press each piece of knitting carefully (see page 44). Backstitch the sleeves into the armholes, as in the basic pattern, then backstitch the underarm and side seams.

You can wear this sweater with the tube skirt on p.22

Contrasting sleeves

To knit this sweater you will need 5 × 50g balls of wool for the body and 4 × 50g balls for two sleeves.

For this one you will need 5 × 50g balls for the body and 2 × 50g balls in two extra colours for each sleeve.

Picture knitting

You can knit a sweater with your initial or a number on it, following the basic sweater pattern on page 20. You will need the same amount of yarn plus one ball in a contrasting colour. Before you start the sweater, make a chart of the picture you want, showing which colour to knit each stitch. Patterns always use charts for multi-coloured knits, as they are easier to follow than written instructions.

Making a chart

You will need:
squared paper
pencil or felt pen
ruler
coloured pencils
your knitting pattern

Decide how big to make the motif, then work out how many stitches and rows it will take up, using the tension for the pattern as a guide. For example, a letter to fit a 10cm square will take up 21 sts and 29 rows. (A 20cm square will take up 42 sts and 58 rows).

On the squared paper draw a rectangle 21 squares across and 29 squares high. Each square represents a stitch and each line a row. Then draw your letter or number to fit in the rectangle. Keep the shape bold and step the curves to fit the grid. Then lightly colour it in.

Following a chart

From a chart you can see straightaway which colour to knit every stitch. Starting at the bottom you read from right to left for a knit row and from left to right for a purl row. Laying a ruler across the chart below the row you are knitting will help you to keep your place as you go along.

Chart for a number

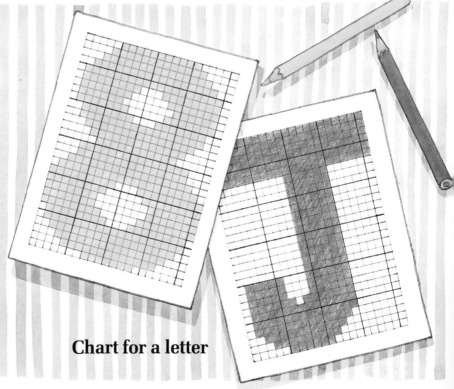

Chart for a letter

Where to put the motif

From the measurements of the sweater, decide where to put the motif. It is easiest to knit it before you start the armhole shaping. If you want the motif to be in the centre of the sweater, work out from the pattern how many stitches there should be on either side of it.

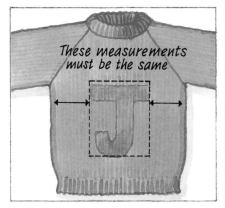

These measurements must be the same

Knitting the motif

For the letter J you need two balls of wool in the main colour and one in the contrasting colour.* Following the chart, knit as far as the first stitch of the motif in the main colour. Join the contrast colour, leaving a loose end, and knit the number of stitches shown on the chart. Then join the second ball of the main colour and knit to the end of the row.

On the following rows, change the balls of wool for different colour areas, but from now on cross the old colour over the new one when you knit a stitch in a new colour, as shown. This stops you from getting holes where the colours join. Be careful not to tangle the balls of wool.

On a knit row

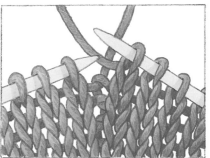

On a purl row

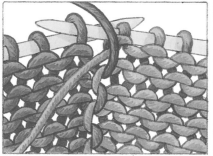

When you have finished the motif, break off the contrast yarn and the extra ends of the main colour. Sew these into the back of the knitting later.

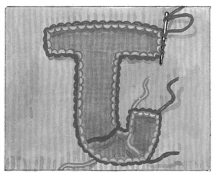

Other pictures

You can design and knit other motifs in the same way as long as you work them out on squared paper first.

Keep your designs simple and do not use too many colours in a row. You need a separate ball of wool for each colour change in any one row, so if there arc two bands of contrast colour, wind a second ball from your ball of contrast wool.

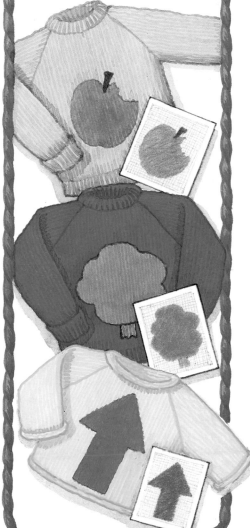

* If your initial or number has two bands of contrast colour, wind a second ball from your ball of contrast colour.

Blue jacket

You will need:
7x 100g balls Icelandic wool

1 pair size
6½ mm needles
2 spare needles

6 2¼ cm diameter buttons

Size

One size to fit 81-87cm (32"-34") chest.

Moss stitch

You can check how to do this on page 10. The tension is 14 sts and 24 rows to 10cm, using size 6½mm needles.

Back

With size 6½mm needles cast on 66 sts and knit 8 rows garter st (knit every row). Then change to moss st and continue until work measures 52cm from beginning. Cast off 21 sts at beginning of the next 2 rows and leave remaining 24 sts on a spare needle.

This chunky jacket is made in moss stitch with garter stitch borders

Pockets

Make 2 pockets. For each one cast on 14 sts and work 10cm in moss st. Leave both the pockets on spare needles.

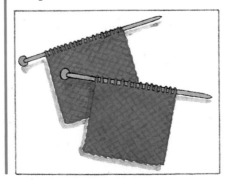

Left front

Cast on 36 sts and knit 8 rows garter st, then continue in moss st until work measures 13cm from beginning.

Adding the pocket

Continuing in moss st, work 5 sts, then cast off 14 sts. Knit the 14 sts at the top of one of the pockets, then continue to end of row (check that you have not made any mistakes in the moss st). Push the pocket flap to the wrong side of the knitting.

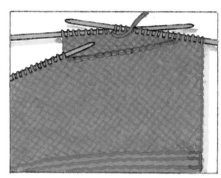

Continue straight until work measures 45cm from beginning.

Neck shaping

At beginning of next row on wrong side of knitting (the neck edge) cast off 7 sts. Continuing in moss st, decrease 1 st at neck edge on next 2 rows, then 1 st on every alternate row until there are 21 sts left.

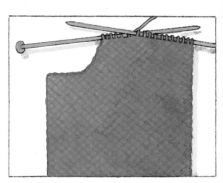

Continue straight until work measures 52cm from beginning. Cast off remaining sts loosely.

Right front

Cast on 36 sts and work 8 rows in garter st, then make the 1st buttonhole.

Making a buttonhole

Row 1 Work 3 sts in moss st, cast off 2 sts, then continue to end of row.
Row 2 Work 31 sts in moss st up to cast off sts, turn knitting, cast on 2 sts, turn knitting back and continue to end of row.

You have to make 6 buttonholes like this up the jacket front. Space them 8cm apart. The last buttonhole should come about 2cm before you start to shape the neck.

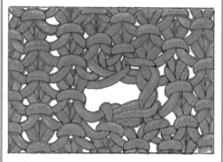

Continue straight, making buttonholes where needed, until you have knitted 13cm moss st, then knit in the pocket:
Next row Moss st 17, cast off 14 then knit the 14 at the top of the pocket in moss st, and moss st to end of row. Continue straight until work measures 45cm from beginning, ending with a wrong side row.

Shape neck

Cast off 7 sts at beginning of next row, then continue in moss st, decreasing 1 st at neck edge on next 2 rows, then every alternate row until there are 21 sts left. Continue straight until work measures 52cm from beginning, then cast off loosely.

Sleeves

Cast on 30 sts. Work 8 rows in garter st, then continue in moss st. Increase* 1 st at each end of the row every 2cm until you have 64 sts. Continue straight until work measures 42cm. Work 8 rows of garter st, then cast off loosely.

Measurements

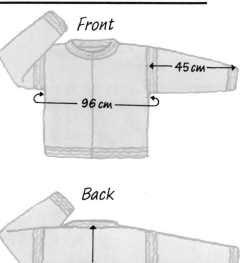

Front

←— 45 cm —→

←——— 96 cm ———→

Back

55 cm

32 cm

---

*You can check how to increase on page 42.

Blue jacket 2

Making up

Pin each piece of knitting out to the right measurements, right side down* and gently press it on the wrong side.

Sew up the shoulder seams with flat seams.

Neckband

Pick up the stitches for the neckband with the right side of the knitting facing you. Start at the neck edge of the right Front.

Pick up the 7 cast off sts, then 14 sts up to the shoulder, spacing them evenly**. Knit up the 24 sts at the top of the Back, then pick up 14 sts down the side of the left Front neck and the 7 cast off sts to the centre Front. You should have 66 sts altogether. Knit 4 rows garter st, then cast off loosely.

Pin the backs of the pockets flat against the wrong side of the Front pieces and oversew round the 3 free sides.

Measure 23cm down the Back and Front from the shoulder seams and sew in marker threads in a contrasting colour. Pin the sleeves into the armholes between the marker threads and sew them in with flat seams.

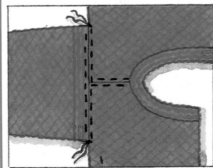

Matching underarm seams, flat seam sleeve and side seams and press seams lightly.

Buttons

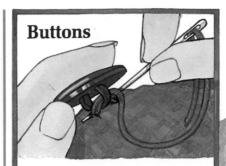

Plain buttons look best on this jacket. They can be in a matching or contrasting colour. Buttons with a shank are best for chunky knits like this.

Positioning the buttons

You must sew the buttons in the right place and in a straight line, or they will spoil the look of the jacket. Lay the buttonhole edge of the jacket over the edge of the left front by about 4cm, so the buttonholes cover the edge. Make sure the top and bottom edges of the jacket match and keep the buttonhole edge straight. Mark where the centre of each buttonhole comes with a pin, to show where to sew on the buttons.

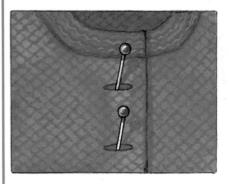

When you have sewn on the buttons, check that they are in the right place. They should be about 2cm in from the edge of the jacket.

Zip-up jacket

Jacket with collar and zip down the front

Instead of buttons you will need an open-ended zip the same length as the finished Front (approximately 45cm). It is better to buy a zip that is slightly too short rather than one which is too long, so you can ease it into place without stretching the edges of the knitting.

Follow the basic pattern for the jacket, only leave out the buttonholes on the right Front. To add a collar to the jacket, knit 10cm garter st instead of 8 rows for the neckband, then fold it over.

Sewing in the zip

Keep the zip closed and pin it to the wrong side of the Front opening. The edges of the knitting should be very close to the teeth and the right and left Front should match at the top and bottom.

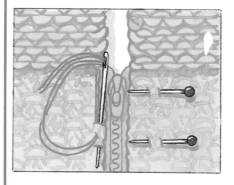

Using a sewing needle and a double strand of sewing thread in a matching colour, backstitch one side of the zip firmly in place. Start at the top and work down to the bottom, sewing about 2 sts in from the edge of the jacket. Do the same on the other side. Turn the jacket inside out, tuck in the top ends of the zip and sew them down.

Different yarns

You can knit this jacket in other types of chunky wool, as long as the yarn labels recommend the same size needles. Check the tension before you start, to make sure the jacket ends up the right size.

You could also knit it in a mohair that recommends the same needle size. Mohair should be knitted loosely and you must not press it.

Aran sweater

You will need:
14 (15) × 50g balls of Aran wool

1 pair size 4mm needles

1 pair size 5mm needles

1 stitch holder

1 cable needle

Aran knitting

Aran sweaters have a very patterned surface with cables and several different types of stitch on them. They were first knitted in the Aran islands, off the coast of Ireland, by the wives of the fishermen. Each type of stitch or cable had its own meaning and the women made up their own patterns.

Traditionally the sweaters are knitted in natural coloured wool, like the sweater here.

This sweater looks complicated but is quite easy. You can make it with either a polo neck or a crew neck.

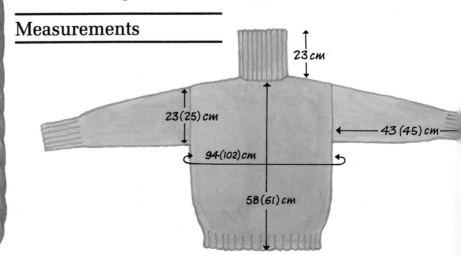

Tension

18 sts and 24 rows = 10cm in dbl moss st, using 5mm needles.

Size

One size to fit 81-87cm (32-34 inch) chest.

Measurements

23 cm

23 (25) cm

43 (45) cm

94 (102) cm

58 (61) cm

There are only three different kinds of stitch used in this pattern: ribbing, double moss stitch and cables.

You can find out how to do double moss stitch and cables for the sweater on this page, and the pattern starts on the next page.

Double moss stitch

Row 1 k2, p2 to last 2 sts, k2.
Row 2 p2, k2 to last 2 sts, p2.
Row 3 p2, k2 to last 2 sts, p2.
Row 4 k2, p2 to last 2 sts, k2.
Rep these 4 rows throughout.

What does m1 mean?

For Row 1, where it says m1, it means make a new stitch by increasing between the stitches. You can find out how to do this on p.42.

Knitting cables

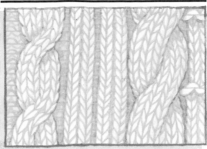

When you knit a cable, you cross one group of stitches first over, then behind, another group of stitches. You use a cable needle to hold the first group of stitches out of the way until you want to knit them. Always use a cable needle the same size or smaller than the other needles you are using so it does not stretch the stitches.

In this pattern there are cables 4 stitches wide and 8 stitches wide. They are both knitted in the same way; you just slip more stitches on to the cable needle to make the wider cable. Here you can find out how to knit a cable 4 stitches wide.

Cable that twists to the left

Slip 2 stitches on to the cable needle and hold them at the front of the knitting, then knit the next 2 stitches.

Now knit the 2 stitches from the cable needle.

Cable that twists to the right

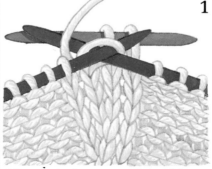

Slip 2 stitches on to the cable needle and hold them at the back of the knitting, then knit the next 2 stitches.

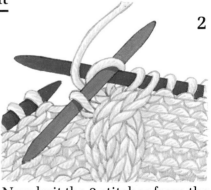

Now knit the 2 stitches from the cable needle.

Aran sweater 2

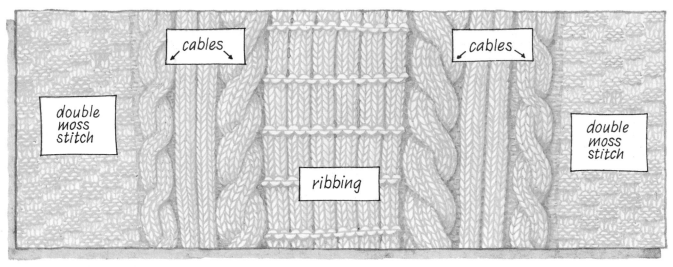

double moss stitch

cables

cables

ribbing

double moss stitch

Back

Cast on 80(86) sts on size 4mm needles and work k2, p2 rib for 7cm.

Increase row Rib 8(7), m1 * rib 4, m1 ** to the last 8(7) sts, rib to the end of the row – 97(105) sts.

Change to size 5mm needles and start the Aran pattern as follows. The pattern has 16 rows which you keep repeating. By the time you have knitted them once, you will find it much easier to follow.

Aran pattern

Row 1 Double moss st 14(18), p2, k4, p2, k2, p2, k2, p2, k8, p2, (k2, p1) 5 times, k2, p2, k8, p2, k2, p2, k2, p2, k4, p2, double moss st 14(18).

Row 2 Double moss st 14(18), k2, p4, k2, p2, k2, p2, k2, p8, k2, (p2, k1) 5 times, p2, k2, p8, k2, p2, k2, p2, k2, p4, k2, double moss st 14(18).

Row 3 Repeat row 1.

Row 4 Repeat row 2.

Row 5 Double moss st 14(18), p2, slip 2 sts on to cable needle at front of work, k2, k2 sts from cable needle, p2, k2, p2, k2, p2, k8, p2, (k2, p1) 5 times, k2, p2, k8, p2, k2, p2, k2, p2, slip 2 sts on to cable needle at back of work, k2, k2 sts from cable needle, p2, double moss st 14(18).

Row 6 Repeat row 2.

Row 7 Double moss st 14 (18), p2, k4, p2, k2, p2, k2, p2, slip 4 sts on to cable needle at front of work, k4, k4 sts from cable needle, p21, slip 4 sts on to cable needle at back of work, k4, k4 sts from cable needle, p2, k2, p2, k2, p2, k4, p2, double moss st 14(18).

Row 8 Repeat row 2.
Row 9 Repeat row 3.
Row 10 Repeat row 2.
Row 11 Repeat row 3.
Row 12 Repeat row 2.
Row 13 Repeat row 5.

Row 14 Repeat row 2.
Row 15 Repeat row 7.
Row 16 Repeat row 2.

Repeat the 16 rows of pattern until knitting measures 58(61)cm from beginning.

Shaping shoulders

Next row Cast off 32(36) sts at beginning of row, slip next 33 sts on to a stitch holder, cast off last 32(36)sts.

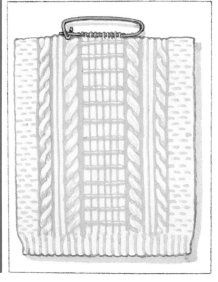

Front

Repeat as for Back until work measures 47 (54)cm from beginning.

Shaping the neck

Work 40(43)sts in Aran pattern and slip rest of stitches on to a stitch holder. Continue left shoulder in pattern on the stitches already knitted, decreasing 1st at beginning of every wrong side row until there are 32 (36) sts left.

Continue straight in pattern until work measures 58(61)cm, then cast off loosely.

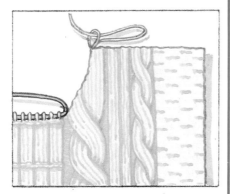

Leave centre 17 sts on a stitch holder and knit right shoulder on remaining sts. Continuing in pattern, cast off 1 st at the beginning of right side rows until there are 32(36) sts left. Continue as for left shoulder.

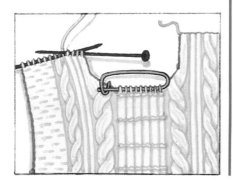

Sleeves

Cast on 36(38) sts on size 4mm needles and work k2, p2 rib for 14cm.

Next row Increase 24(26) sts as follows: (k1, m1), k1, m1, k1, m1, k1, * k1, m1, k1, m1, k2, m1, k2, m1 **, repeat from * to ** to the last 3(4) sts, (k1, m1), k1, m1, k1, m1, k1.

Row 1 (K2), p2, k4, p2, k2, p2, k2, p2, k8, p2, k2, p1, k2, p1, k2, p2, k8, p2, k2, p2, k2, p2, k4, p2, (k2).

Row 2 (P2), k2, p4, k2, p2, k2, p2, k2, p8, k2, p2, k1, p2, k1, p2, k2, p8, k2, p2, k2, p2, k2, p4, k2, (p2).

Row 3 (K2), p2, k4, p2, k2, p2, k2, p2, k8, p2, k2, p1, k2, p1, k2, p2, k8, p2, k2, p2, k2, p2, k4, p2, (k2).

Row 4 Repeat row 2.

Row 5 (K2), p2, slip 2 sts on to cable needle at front of work, k2, k2 sts from cable needle, p2, k2, p2, k2, p2, k8, p2, k2, p1, k2, p1, k2, p2, k8, p2, k2, p2, k2, p2, slip 2 sts on to cable needle at back of work, k2, k2 sts from cable needle, p2 (k2).

Row 6 Repeat row 2.

Row 7 (k2), p2, k4, p2, k2, p2, k2, p2, slip 4 sts on to cable needle at front of work, k4, k4 sts from cable needle, p12, slip 4 sts on to cable needle at back of work, k4, k4 sts from cable needle, p2, k2, p2, k2, p2, k4, p2(k2).

Row 8 Repeat row 2.
Row 9 Repeat row 3.

Row 10 Repeat row 2.
Row 11 Repeat row 3.
Row 12 Repeat row 2.
Row 13 Repeat row 5.
Row 14 Repeat row 2.
Row 15 Repeat row 7.
Row 16 Repeat row 2.

Following Aran pattern, increase 1 st at each end of a right side row every 2.5cm until there are 86 (92)sts. Knit the new sts in double moss st. When you have finished increasing, you should have 14(17)sts in double moss st on each side of the sleeve. Continue straight until work measures 50(52)cm from beginning. Cast off.

Keeping your place

Use a row counter and mark where you are up to on the pattern, so that you do not lose your place.

Aran sweater 3

Polo neck

You knit the neck for this sweater before you sew it up, as for the pink sweater on page 24. This makes it easier to sew up the sweater.

With the right side of the work facing you, pick up the stitches for the neck with a size 4mm needle. You can find out how to do this at the bottom of page 26. Knit across the 33 sts at the top of the Back, then pick up 18 sts down the left side of Front neck, 17 sts across the centre of the neck and 18 sts up the right side of neck. You should have 86 sts altogether.

With size 4mm needles, work k2, p2 rib for 23cm. Cast off.

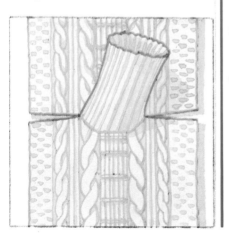

Pressing

Pin each piece of knitting in turn out to the correct size, right side down (see page 27). Lightly press the pieces on the wrong side (but do not press the ribbing).

Making up

Measure 23(25)cm down from the shoulders and make tacks in coloured thread to show where to sew in the sleeves.

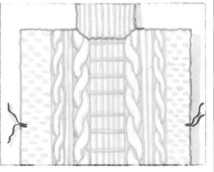

Lay the Back and Front right sides together and backstitch the shoulder seams. Open the sweater out and pin and backstitch the sleeves in place between the tacks.

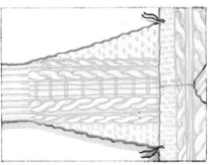

Backstitch the sleeve underarm seams and the side seams as far as the cuffs and ribbing. Sew up the cuffs, ribbing and polo neck with flat seams. Fold the cuffs back and the polo neck down.

Crew neck sweater

To knit a ribbed crew neck instead of a polo neck, follow the instructions for picking up the neck sts, but only knit 6cm in k2, p2 rib. Leave the stitches on the needle, then fold the neckband in half to the wrong side of the knitting and loosely sew each stitch in turn to the first row of the neck ribbing. You can find out how to do this on page 26.

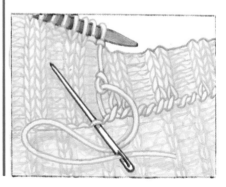

Making your knitting fit

Before you start knitting anything for yourself, take your measurements so that you know which size to knit. All the patterns in this book have been designed to fit sizes 10 and 12.

Below you can see which measurements you need to take for most knitting patterns. The chart to the right shows you the standard measurements for sizes 10 and 12.

Size chart

Metric			Imperial		
10		**12**	**10**		**12**
83cm	chest	87cm	32½"	chest	34"
64cm	waist	67cm	25"	waist	26½"
88cm	hips	92cm	34½"	hips	36"

Taking measurements

Chest

Length of back from nape of neck to waist

Under arm to wrist

What is ease?

Too tight

Too loose

Most knitting patterns are designed to allow some 'ease'. This means that the garment is not skin tight, but allows room for movement. For example a sweater for someone with a size 32" chest will actually measure 34" around the chest.

Altering the length

Make longer or shorter here

If you want your sweater to be longer or shorter than it says in the pattern, work out what measurement you want it to be up to the armhole and alter the length before shaping the armhole. You alter the length of sleeves in the same way.

Increasing stitches

Increasing and decreasing the number of stitches on your needles are ways of shaping your knitting. Knitting patterns always tell you when to increase or decrease, but not usually how to do it. On these two pages you can find out.

You usually only increase stitches on a knit row. There are two basic ways to do this.

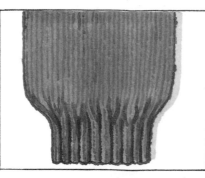

Where a pattern tells you to increase several stitches across a row, at the top of ribbing for example, it is best to increase between the stitches.

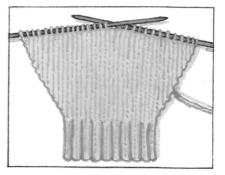

If the pattern tells you to increase at each end of a row, when knitting a sleeve for example, increase by knitting twice into the same stitch.

Increasing between stitches

Pick up the thread between the two stitches on the row below with your left needle.

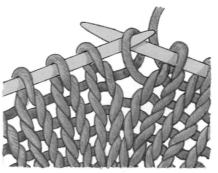

Now knit into the back of the loop. This twists the stitch so it does not make a hole.

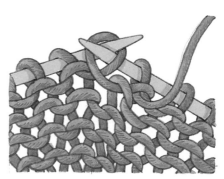

On a purl row, purl into the back of the loop, as shown.

Knitting twice into the same stitch

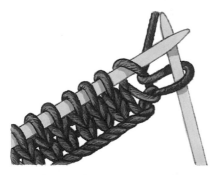

Knit into the stitch in the usual way, but do not slip it off the left needle.

Then knit into the back of the same stitch, to make two stitches, and carry on as usual.

At the end of a row, knit twice into the second-to-last stitch, not the last one. This gives your knitting a more even edge.

How to decrease stitches

You decrease stitches to make knitting narrower, for example when shaping armholes. Patterns usually tell you to decrease one stitch at each end of a row. The easiest way to do this is to knit or purl two stitches together. Some people find it better not to include the first or last stitches in a row because this can make the edge of the knitting uneven.

Knitting 2 stitches together

Put the right needle into two stitches, as shown, and knit them together as if they were one stitch.

Purling 2 stitches together

Put the right needle into two stitches, as shown, and purl them together as if they were one stitch.

Neat armholes

When you knit 2 stitches together, they slant either to the right or left. If you are shaping a raglan armhole it looks best if the stitches slant in the same direction as the edge of the knitting.

Knitting or purling stitches together on the right side of stocking stitch makes them slant to the right. To make stitches slant to the left, knit them together through the back of the stitches.

Knitting stitches together through the back of the stitches

Put the right needle through the back loops of two stitches, as shown, and knit them together.

Purling stitches together through the back of the stitches

Put the right needle through the backs of two stitches, as shown, and purl them together.

Making the stitches slant the right way

decrease edge

decrease edge

On a knit row, k2 tog through the back of the stitches at the beginning of the row and k2 tog at the end of the row.

On a purl row, p2 tog at the beginning of the row and p2 tog through the back of the stitches at the end of the row.

Finishing off your knitting

To make your knitting look professional, you must finish it off carefully.

You will need:

iron

pressing cloth

darning needle

pins

leftover yarn

tape measure

How to measure your knitting

Measure your knitting as you do it, to make sure each piece is the right size, or you will have problems sewing it up.

Lay the knitting flat on a table or the floor, making sure you do not stretch it. Measure straight up the middle of it, not up one of the edges.

Pressing

Pressing knitting makes it look more even and 'finished'. Only press your knitting if the pattern tells you to, as many synthetic yarns should not be pressed at all. Check the yarn label too, just to make sure. On the chart below you can see what the different ironing symbols mean.

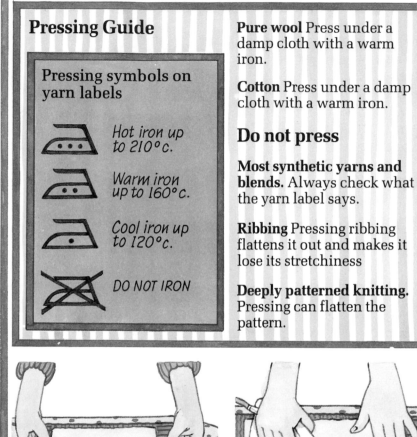

Pressing Guide

Pressing symbols on yarn labels

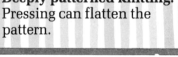

Hot iron up to 210°c.

Warm iron up to 160°c.

Cool iron up to 120°c.

DO NOT IRON

Pure wool Press under a damp cloth with a warm iron.

Cotton Press under a damp cloth with a warm iron.

Do not press

Most synthetic yarns and blends. Always check what the yarn label says.

Ribbing Pressing ribbing flattens it out and makes it lose its stretchiness

Deeply patterned knitting. Pressing can flatten the pattern.

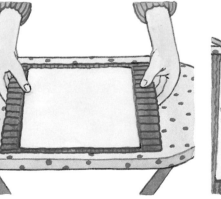

Turn the iron on to the right temperature. Always press knitting on the wrong side, so lay it, right side down, on the ironing board. Cover the knitting with a damp cloth. Gently lay the iron on it for a few seconds, then lift it up.

Do not move the iron around as you usually do. Press all of the knitting evenly in this way, a bit at a time. Try not to press so hard that you flatten the knitting. Let it dry properly, then sew it up.

Sewing up your knitting

Knitting patterns always tell you in what order to sew up your knitting. The patterns in this book also tell you what kind of seam to use. The most useful types of seam are the flat seam and the backstitch seam.

Sew up seams with the knitting yarn and a tapestry or darning needle. If your yarn is very thick, use a 4 ply yarn the same colour instead.

Sewing in yarn ends

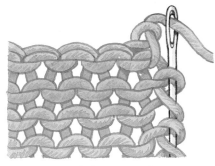

Thread each loose end in turn on to a darning needle and sew it neatly into a seam or the back of the knitting, to hold it firm.

Trim any extra yarn close to the knitting. If you have used more than one colour, sew each loose end into its own colour area.

Backstitch

Backstitch can be used for most seams but it makes a ridge and should not be used for ribbing.

Pin the two pieces right sides together, matching the row ends if possible. Start off with a couple of small stiches, one on top of the other, then sew the seam as shown, from right to left. Sew in the yarn firmly at the end of the seam with a couple of small stitches.

1

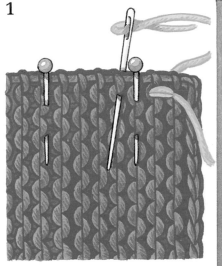

2

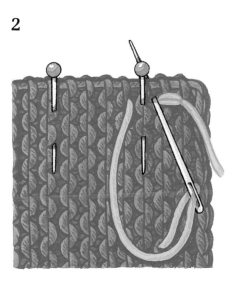

3

Flat seaming

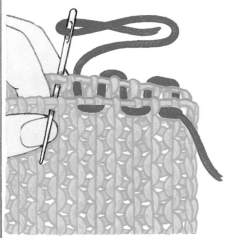

Use this for sewing up ribbing and things you have knitted with thick yarn.

Put the knitting right sides together, matching the rows if you are sewing up a straight edge. Put your left forefinger between the two pieces of knitting and join the yarn with a couple of stitches. Sew the seam, as shown, being careful not to sew too tightly. Finish it off as for backstitch.

45

Putting mistakes right

Unfortunately when you knit, things go wrong from time to time. Do not despair. It is easy to put mistakes right and does not take long.

Every knitter drops a stitch from time to time. Here you can find out how to pick up dropped stitches on both knit and purl rows.

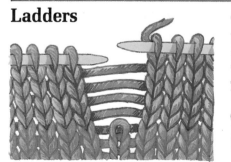

Picking up a dropped knit stitch

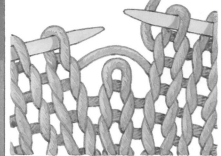

This is what a dropped knit stitch looks like.

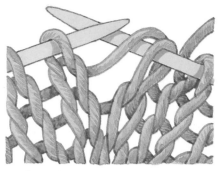

Pick up both the dropped stitch and the loop above it with your right needle, as shown.

Picking up a dropped purl stitch

This is what a dropped purl stitch looks like.

Use your right needle to pick up both the dropped stitch and the loop above it, as shown.

Ladders

If you leave a dropped stitch, it unravels for several rows and makes a ladder. The easiest way to put this right is to pick up the stitches with a crochet hook.

On a knit row

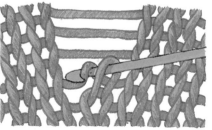

Put the crochet hook through the front of the dropped stitch. Hook up the loop above it and pull it through the stitch to make a new stitch. Carry on like this to the top of the ladder.

On a purl row

Put the crochet hook through the back of the dropped stitch. Hook up a loop and pull it through the stitch to make a new one. Put the hook in again to make each new stitch.

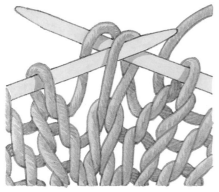

Put the tip of your left needle from back to front into the stitch only.

Lift it over the loop and off the needle, to make a new stitch on the right needle.

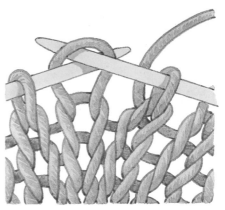

Slip the new stitch on to the left needle, so it is the right way round, as shown.

Put the tip of your left needle from front to back into the stitch only.

Lift the stitch over the loop so that you have a new stitch on the right needle.

Slip the new stitch on to the left needle, as shown.

Unpicking mistakes

If you have made a mistake further back in a row, do not pull the knitting off the needles. Unpick one stitch at a time until you reach the mistake.

Knit stitches

Put the left needle into the stitch below the 1st stitch on the right needle and drop the 1st stitch off the right needle. Repeat along the row, keeping the yarn at the back of the work.

Purl stitches

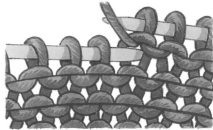

Put the left needle purlwise into the stitch below the 1st stitch on the right needle and drop the 1st stitch off the right needle. Repeat along the row, keeping the yarn to the front.

Index

The yarns used to make the clothes in this book were supplied by the Yarn Store, 8 Ganton Street, London W1.

First published in 1985 by Usborne Publishing Ltd, 83-85 Saffron Hill, London EC1N 8RT, England. Copyright © 1991, 1985 Usborne Publishing Ltd.

The name Usborne and device ♥ are Trade Marks of Usborne Publishing Ltd. All rights reserved.

Printed in Belgium